Can You Imagine?

Bernard J. Weiss
Senior Author
Reading and Linguistics

Susan B. Cruikshank
Reading and Language Arts

Eldonna L. Evertts
Language Arts

Loreli Olson Steuer
Reading and Linguistics

Lyman C. Hunt
General Editor—Satellite Books

Holt
Basic
Reading

Level 6

HOLT, RINEHART AND WINSTON, PUBLISHERS
New York • Toronto • Mexico City • London • Sydney • Tokyo

ISBN 0-03-061387-6
345   071   9876543

Acknowledgments:

Grateful acknowledgment is given to the following authors and publishers:

Doubleday & Company, Inc., for "Conversation," from *Fifty-One New Nursery Rhymes*, by Rose Fyleman. Copyright 1932 by Doubleday & Company, Inc. Used by permission.

Harcourt Brace Jovanovich, Inc., for "Good Morning, Cat" from *Wide Awake and Other Poems*. Copyright © 1959 by Myra Cohn Livingston. Used by permission.

Lothrop, Lee & Shepard Co., Inc., for "A Good House," adapted from *The Mitten* by Alvin Tresselt. Copyright © 1964 by Lothrop, Lee & Shepard Co., Inc. Used by permission.

Western Publishing Company, for "A Bear's Life" by Orissa Rines from *Story Parade* Magazine. Copyright 1953 by Story Parade, Inc. Used by permission.

Art Credits:

Tim and Greg Hildebrandt, pages 4 – 13
Ray Cruz, pages 14 – 15, 51
Aaron Heller, pages 16 – 25
Lorraine Fox, pages 26 – 32
Marilyn Bass Goldman, page 33
Karl W. Stücklen, pages 34 – 41
Harry Rosenbaum, pages 42, 62 – 63
Gilbert Riswold, pages 43 – 50
Neil Waldman, pages 52 – 61
Cover art by James Endicott

Table of Contents

A Good House

A mouse saw a blue mitten.

He ran up to it.

"What a good house," said the mouse.

"What a good house for a mouse,"
he said.

And in he went.

A little frog saw the mitten.
He ran up to it.
"What a good house for a frog,"
he said.

"Come in," said the mouse.
"You will like it in here."

And in went the frog.

A pig saw the blue mitten.

He ran up to it.

"What a good house for a pig,"
he said.

"Come in," said the mouse again.

In went the pig with the mouse
and the frog.

A wolf ran up to the blue mitten.
"What a good house for a wolf,"
he said.

"Come in," said the mouse again.

In went the wolf with the mouse
and the frog and the pig.

A sheep saw the blue mitten.
"What a good house for a sheep,"
she said.

"Come in," said the mouse again.

In went the sheep with the mouse
and the frog and the pig and the wolf.

A bear saw the blue mitten.
"What a good house for a bear,"
he said.

"Come in," said the mouse again.

In went the bear with the mouse
and the frog and the pig and the wolf
and the sheep.

A bee saw the blue mitten.

"What a good house for a bee,"
he said.

"Can I come in with you?"

"No!" said the mouse.

"Stop!" said the frog.

In went the bee.
Pop went the mitten!
Out went the mouse and the frog
and the pig and the wolf
and the sheep and the bear
and the bee!

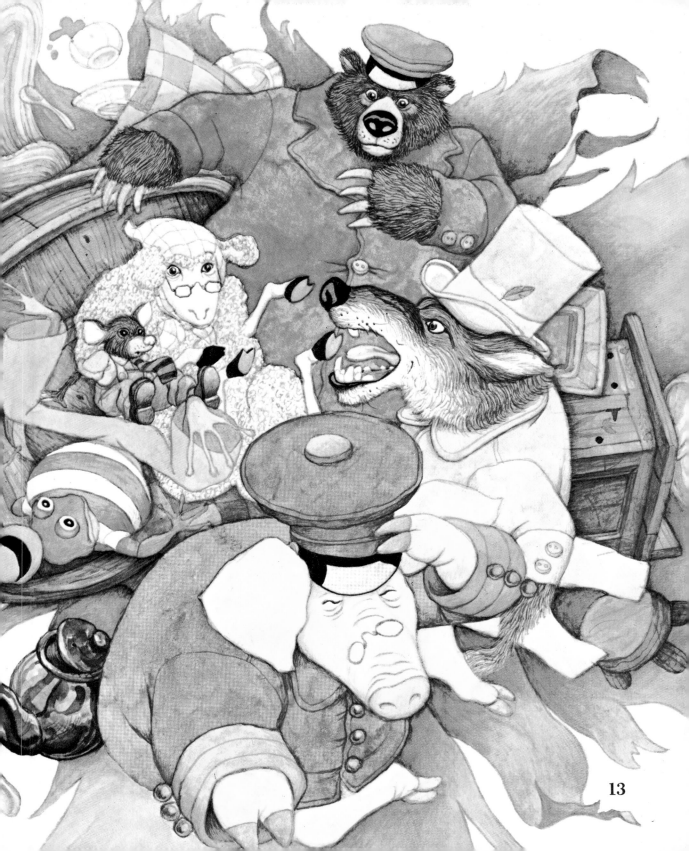

Conversation

"Mousie, mousie,
Where is your little wee housie?"

"Here is the door,
Under the floor,"
Said mousie, mousie.

"Mousie, mousie,
May I come into your housie?"

14

"You can't get in,
You have to be thin,"
Said mousie, mousie.

"Mousie, mousie,
Won't you come out
of your housie?"

"I'm sorry to say,
I'm busy all day,"
Said mousie, mousie.

—Rose Fyleman

15

City Mouse, Country Mouse

A city mouse came to the country.

He came to see the country mouse.

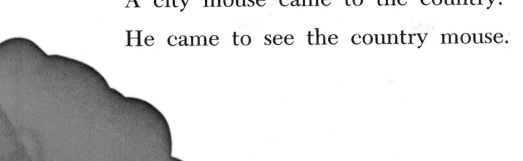

"Come in, come in,"
said the country mouse.
"It is good to see you.
You will like it here."

"What do you eat?"
asked the city mouse.

"I eat beans and water,"
said the country mouse.
"I will get beans for you."

The city mouse didn't like beans.

He didn't like the little house.

He didn't like the country.

"Come with me to the city.

You will like it," said the city mouse.

The country mouse went
with the city mouse.
They came to the city.
They saw a big house.

"Here is my house,"
said the city mouse.
"Come in.
I will find cookies to eat."

The city mouse went to find cookies.

He saw big and little cookies.

"Come here," he said.

"Come and eat the cookies."

The country mouse ran to eat.

He did not get cookies in the country.

"What good cookies," he said.

A cat came into the house.
He saw the city mouse
and the country mouse.

The city mouse saw the cat.
"A cat!" he said.
And out he ran.

The country mouse ran out
with the city mouse.

"Good-by," said the country mouse.
"The city is not for me.
I like the big house.
I like the good cookies.
But I do not like the cat."

23

The country mouse ran to his house.
"I like my country house," he said.

And he didn't go to the city again.

A Bear Like Me

Jimmy was a little boy,
and Teddy was his bear.
One night Teddy ran out.

"I want a bear to play with,"
Teddy said.
"I want to find a bear like me."

Teddy saw a little house.

He went in.

He saw a dog.

"Hello," said Teddy.

"What do you want?" asked the dog.

"A bear like me," said Teddy.

"You won't find a bear in here!
Good night!" said the dog.

Teddy saw a big house.

He went in.

He saw three sheep.

"Hello," said Teddy.

"What do you want?"
asked the sheep.

"A bear like me," said Teddy.

"You won't find a bear in here!
Good night!" said the sheep.

Teddy saw a cow.

"Hello," said Teddy.

"What do you want?" asked the cow.

"A bear like me," said Teddy.

"You won't find a bear in here.
Good night!" said the cow.

Teddy ran out.

He saw a bear.

It was a **big** bear!

It was not like Teddy.

"Stop," said the big bear.

"What do you want?"

"I want to find a bear like me,"
said Teddy.
"You are a big bear.
You are not like me.
Good night and good-by!"

31

Teddy ran to Jimmy.

"I like to play with Jimmy," he said.
"Big bears are not like me!"

A Bear's Life

A Bear takes life quite easy
As a rule.
In Fall he just trots off to bed
Instead of school.

—Orissa Rines

Who Will Get the Apples?

34

Two pigs saw a big tree.

"Do you see what I see?"
asked the big pig.

"Apples!" said the little pig.
"I see apples on the tree!"

"Two apples," said the big pig.
"One is for you, and one is for me."

"Can you get the apples?"
asked the little pig.

"No," said the big pig.
"Can you?"

"No," said the little pig.
"Who can get the apples?"

"The wolf can," said the big pig.
"And here he comes."

"Hello, Wolf," said the big pig.

"Do you see the apples on the tree?

Will you get one for me

and one for my brother?"

"No," said the wolf.

"I won't get apples for you.

I will get apples for me."

The wolf went up the tree.

"I will trick the wolf,"
said the big pig to his brother.
"He won't eat the apples.
But you will see.
I will make the wolf get the apples
for you and me."

38

"Wolf," said the big pig.
"I can jump up and down.
Can you jump?" he asked.

"I can jump," said the wolf.
"See me?"

"I see you," said the big pig.

39

The wolf went up and down,
 up and down,
  up and down.

The apples went up and down,
 up and down,
  up and down,
   down, down.

"What a good trick!"
said the little pig.
"Here come the apples!"

The wolf didn't see the pigs.

He didn't see the apples come down.

The pigs ran with the apples.

And the wolf went up and down,

    up and down,

        up and down.

41

If I Were an Apple

If I were an apple
And grew on a tree,
I think I'd fall down
On a nice boy like me.

I wouldn't stay there
Giving nobody joy:
I'd fall down at once,
And say, "Eat me, my boy!"

42

Who Will Play?

"I want to play," said the cat.
"The little boy likes to play.
He will play with me."

The cat ran to the little boy.

"No, no, cat," said the little boy.
"I do not want to play with you.
I want to play with my game."

The cat ran out.

"The little girl likes to play,"
said the cat.
"She will play with me."

The cat ran up to the girl.

"No, no, cat," said the little girl.
"I do not want to play with you.
I want to read my book."

The cat ran to the mouse house.

"Mouse, mouse," said the cat.
"Come on out.
Come out and play with me."

"No," said the mouse.
"I will not play with a cat."

The cat saw the goldfish.
He ran to the goldfish.

"Hello," said the cat.
"Will you play with me?"

"No," said the goldfish.
"I will not play with a cat."

"Who will play with me?"
asked the cat.

"I will," said the big dog.
He ran to the cat.

"I will play with the little boy,"
said the cat.
"I will play with the little girl.
I will play with the goldfish
and the mouse.
But I will **not** play with a dog!"

Out ran the cat.

And up a tree he went!

50

Good Morning, Cat

Good morning, cat,
you're in my yard
and sniffing for a mouse;
you might as well give up — because
he's hiding in the house.

—Myra Cohn Livingston

51

The Big City

A cow went down a country road.
She saw a frog in the road.

"Hello, little frog," said the cow.
"I want to go to the city.
I want to see big stores.
I want to see cars and big houses.
Where is the city?"

"Here is a sign," said the frog.
"It says where to go.
Can you read it?"

"No," said the cow.

54

"I will read the sign for you,"
said the frog.
"It says, 'To the City.'
Go down the road.
You will find the city."

55

The cow went down the road.

She saw a sign on a tree.

And she saw three sheep.

"Who can read the sign?"
asked the cow.
"I want to find the city."

Beans 20¢

"I can read the sign,"
said the big sheep.
"It says, 'To the City.'
Go down the road,
and you will find the city."

The cow went down the road.

She didn't see the city.

But she saw a big sign.

"Where is the city?"
she asked a mouse.

"Can you read the sign for me?"

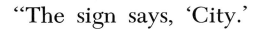

"The sign says, 'City.'
You are in the city," said the mouse.

"The city!" said the cow.
"But where are the big stores?
Where are the cars and big houses?"

"Go down the road," said the mouse.
"And you will see the big city."

Country
Store

The cow went down the road.

What did the cow see?

She did not see the city!

But she did see a sign.

"The frog can't read," said the cow.

"The big sheep can't read.

And the mouse can't read."

60

"Who can read?" asked the cow.
"Who can read the sign?
Can someone read the sign for me?"

A little girl came out from the store.
"I can read!" said the girl.
"I can read the sign for you."

And she did.

Stringing Words

blue	apples	Jimmy
good	cat	I
big	brother	you
little	houses	city
	house	tree

	the	a	big	one
no	where	for	into	in

62 Sentence Patterns. Have the children make sentences, using words from the different columns.

is	plays	up	
are	go	down	
want	goes	here	
ran	see	again	
play	saw	out	

two	three	who	what
to	with	and	not

New Words

The words listed beside the page numbers below are introduced in *Can You Imagine?*, Level 6 in the HOLT BASIC READING SERIES. The words printed in italics are easily decoded.

6.	*mouse*		*beans*	35.	tree
	mitten	22.	*cat*	39.	jump
7.	frog	23.	but	53.	*road*
	you	26.	Jimmy		*stores*
12.	*bee*		Teddy		cars
	pop		night		where
16.	city	27.	hello		houses
	country		won't	60.	can't
18.	*eat*	34.	apples		